D0961566

Secrets of
Radiant Health
and Well-Being

J. Donald Walters

Hardbound edition 1995

Copyright © 1995

J. Donald Walters

ISBN 1-56589-038-8
10 9 8 7 6 5 4 3 2 1

Photographs: J. Donald Walters
Design: Crystal Clarity Design
Art Direction: Christine Schuppe

Printed in China

CRYSTAL

CLARITY

14618 Tyler Foote Road
Nevada City, CA 95959
1-800-424-1055

A seed thought is offered for every day of the month. Begin a day at the appropriate date. Repeat the saying several times: first out loud, then softly, then in a whisper, and then only mentally. With each repetition, allow the words to become absorbed ever more deeply into your subconscious.

Thus, gradually, you will acquire a complete understanding of each day's thought. At this point, indeed, the truths set forth here will have become your own.

Keep the book open at the pertinent page throughout the day. Refer to it occasionally during moments of leisure. Relate the saying as often as possible to real situations in your life.

Then at night, before you go to bed, repeat the thought several times more. While falling asleep, carry the words into your subconscious, absorbing their positive influence into your whole being. Let it become thereby an integral part of your normal consciousness.

*The secret of radiant health
and well-being is maintaining
a balanced diet.
Eat foods that are rich in vitality.
Study proper food combinations.
Never overeat; rather,
make it a practice
to leave the table feeling
that you could have eaten more.*

DAY ONE

The secret of radiant health and well-being is to eat in a harmonious environment, if possible, and not in places where there is discord and confusion.

DAY TWO

*T*he secret of radiant health
and well-being is
to keep a proper posture:
sit up straight; stand upright;
hold your shoulders back,
your chest up, your chin
parallel to the ground.

DAY THREE

*The secret of radiant health
and well-being is to live
more in your spine.
Your movements and gestures
should flow outward
from that inner center.*

The secret of radiant health
and well-being is proper breathing.
When walking, inhale and exhale
deeply and rhythmically.
As you breathe in, count to four;
hold counting four, exhale to the
same count; hold out four.
Repeat this exercise (4-4-4-4)
six to twelve times. Breathe consciously.
Breathe deeply, from the diaphragm.

DAY FIVE

*The secret of radiant health
and well-being is
exercising to keep fit.
Be conscious of the life-force
flowing in your every movement.*

DAY SIX

*T*he secret of radiant health
and well-being is living
in the awareness that you are energy.
Bear in mind this principle:
"The greater the will,
the greater the flow of energy."
Learn exercises designed to increase
your flow of energy to the body;
practice them regularly.

DAY SEVEN

*The secret of radiant health
and well-being is to practice
some meditation every day.
From your own center of stillness,
send stillness outward
into your entire being.*

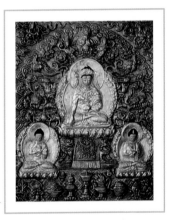

The secret of radiant health
and well-being is to love others –
but impersonally, not with attachment.
Attached love is self-love.
It will tie you inwardly in knots.
But impersonal love brings the body
into perfect harmony.
Pure love develops of itself,
once the pettiness of self-love
has been eradicated with kindness.

DAY NINE

*The secret of radiant health
and well-being is
being happy, within.
Radiate happiness outward with
a sense of total well-being to others.
Happiness is the fruit
of faith in life, in God,
in your own highest potentials.*

*T*he secret of radiant health
and well-being is
to practice willingness.
Train yourself to say
"Yes," where others say
"No," or only "Maybe."

*The secret of radiant health
and well-being is
to keep a positive,
fearless attitude.
By affirming the highest good,
you will attract it
to you always.*

DAY TWELVE

*T*he secret of radiant health
and well-being is to enjoy being
in the fresh air. Breathe more consciously.
With every breath, inhale vitality
and courage into your mind and body;
exhale stale thoughts, discouragement,
and old habit patterns.
Breathe in a sense of inner freedom;
breathe out any lingering sense of bondage.

DAY THIRTEEN

*The secret of radiant health
and well-being is to be relaxed,
both physically and mentally.
Tension holds illness in the body,
whereas relaxation releases
and banishes it. To relax completely,
first tense the body all over;
then exhale forcibly and relax:
Feel the tension leave your body.
Mentally release all your cares and worries
into the receptive vastness of space.*

The secret of radiant health
and well-being is to keep good company.
Mix with generous, energetic,
joyful people – people who are
interested in others and
concerned for their well-being.
Avoid the company of negative people,
or of talking zombies. For the company
you keep can magnetize you, and
can also rob you of your magnetism.

DAY FIFTEEN

*The secret of radiant health
and well-being is
to practice self-control
in all aspects
of your life.
Overindulgence only
wastes vitality.*

DAY SIXTEEN

*T*he secret of radiant health
and well-being is to become
conscious of colors as channels of energy.
Surround yourself with cheerful,
harmonious colors.
Inhale them mentally. Shun dark,
"muddy," or depressing hues.
When selecting foods also, choose
them for their diversity of colors.
Color diversity in food will help ensure
that your diet has the proper balance.

DAY SEVENTEEN

*T*he secret of radiant health
and well-being is to be more conscious
of sounds. When listening to music,
concentrate on the consciousness
that went into its composition. For music,
whether calming or discordant, cheerful or
depressing, affects the entire nervous system.
It can make a person vital and responsive,
or lifeless, dispirited, and resentful.
Give preference to the music of composers
whose awareness, as expressed
through their music, is expansive.

DAY EIGHTEEN

*The secret of radiant health
and well-being is to affirm
good health even in the face of illness.
Positive affirmation
will keep you radiant and strong.
As your inner light shines
brightly from within,
illness will squeeze its eyes
tightly shut and run away.*

DAY NINETEEN

*The secret of radiant health
and well-being is to imagine yourself
surrounded by an aura of light.
Live more in the consciousness
of this light. Expand it mentally.
Include in it the people around you,
the objects, the surrounding space.*

DAY TWENTY

*The secret of radiant health
and well-being is
to transcend self-involvement,
which dulls your consciousness.
Lessen your attachment to pettiness:
to little rules of diet, to little fads.
Expand your consciousness:
Determine to live in inner freedom!*

*The secret of radiant health
and well-being is to be concerned
for others' welfare.
Expand your sympathies
to include others
in your radiant sense
of happiness and well-being.*

*T*he secret of radiant health
and well-being is to practice non-injury.
Our well-being depends
on the kind of thoughts
we hold towards others.
Injurious thoughts steel us
to receive injury ourselves.
Kind thoughts invite
our nervous systems to relax;
they promote self-healing and
offer healing to all whom we meet.

DAY TWENTY-THREE

The secret of radiant health
and well-being is
to practice contentment,
the supreme virtue.
Contentment is the soil
in which all other virtues flourish.
It is a smooth leaf
to which the raindrops
of illness and suffering never cling.

DAY TWENTY-FOUR

The secret of radiant health and
well-being is to practice cleanliness,
inwardly as well as outwardly.
Enjoy wholesome emotions,
good thoughts, worthwhile activities.
Disease thrives where there is impurity.
But we flourish in health
when we pay attention to
cultivating purity – physically,
mentally, emotionally, spiritually.

*T*he secret of radiant health
and well-being is
to practice non-attachment.
Non-attachment bestows inner peace,
the precursor of contentment;
and relaxation,
the consort of good health.

*The secret of radiant health
and well-being is neither
envying anyone nor blaming anyone.
Be at rest in your Self.
Bless all as you proceed
serenely on your way through life.*

DAY TWENTY-SEVEN

*The secret of radiant health
and well-being is to be grateful –
to life; to others.
Gratitude opens windows
to receive the sunlight
of divine abundance.*

DAY TWENTY-EIGHT

*T*he secret of radiant health
and well-being is
to smile in your heart,
even when others scowl.

*T*he secret of radiant health
and well-being is
to become a cause, not an effect.
Let nothing condition your happiness.
Accept from others only what you
choose to accept: their good suggestions,
but not their insistence on them;
their constructive criticisms,
but not their anger. Radiate outward
into the world around you
the light of your faith and wisdom.

DAY THIRTY

The secret of radiant health
and well-being is
to be a friend to all.
When meeting people
for the first time,
think of them as your own.